Critical Acclaim for Josie Di Sciascio-Andrews

"Josie Di Sciascio-Andrews is sure to become one of Canada's most prolific and public poets."

— I.B. Iskov, founder of
The Ontario Poetry Society

"Josie Di Sciascio-Andrews takes the universe, expanding from its zero point and moulds it into a series of poems about intimacy, angst, memory, identity, death — and the hope — the impossible light that keeps us all going."

— Michael Mirolla, Bressani-Prize-
winning author of *The House on 14th Avenue*

"Josie Di Sciascio-Andrews collects memories like she collects sea glass along the shore. It's her quiet polishing of word gems that first drew me to her work. ... In *A Jar of Fireflies*, she continues to collect the past and states that 'memories light up the landscapes of our nights like fireflies.' Themes inspired by her familial remembrances, nature, love, flowers, and dreams dominate this collection. What makes her work shine is her ability to pull in the reader with both her narrative style and sparkling-fresh metaphors."

— Debbie Okun Hill, poet/blogger/freelance
writer, published in *Descant, Existere,
Other Voices, The Literary Review of Canada,
The Windsor Review*, and *Vallum*

"Josie Di Sciascio-Andrews' fifth collection of poems, *A Jar of Fireflies*, is about quests. In particular, it is about the quest in space and time to find a balance, whether recollecting peaceful family life in Italy where Di Sciascio-Andrews grew up, or in her present-day life in Canada. The author's journey concerns the discovery of certain moments of the past to complete her mission in poetry. This is analogical thinking, and her ability to develop not a number of isolated metaphors, but a series of related ones is a natural and inevitable way of exploring the mind/ nature relationship. The external world is internalized and the world of memories is externalized, breaking down borders, as in the work of one of Di Sciascio-Andrews's favourite poets, Pablo Neruda.

One of Di Sciascio-Andrews' strengths lies in the naturally exuberant quality of her voice, expressing itself in an epigrammatic affirmation as in 'Poetic Alchemy': 'I extrapolate wonder from the commonplace' and 'My eyes create reality.' I like these series of interconnected states of wonder, this expression of affirmation and celebration in her work."

— Laurence Hutchman, author of
Swimming Towards the Sun,
Two Maps of Emery, and
Passages/Passaggi

"Traditionally, the poet is understood to articulate a difficult position in society. They are understood to bridge the gap between a political mind, the practical experience, the yearning for improvement, and a burden of disappointments experienced in life with the joy and understanding that emerges through a life connected to people, places, and social events. Di Sciascio-Andrews has directed her poetry toward that function, and she usually achieves her goal."

— Sharon Berg, an author whose work has
appeared in Canada, the United States, Mexico,
the U.K., the Netherlands, India, Singapore,
and Australia

A Jar of Fireflies

Other works by Josie Di Sciascio-Andrews

Poetry:
The Whispers of Stones
Sea Glass
The Red Accordion
Letters from the Singularity
Sunrise Over Lake Ontario
Meta Stasis

Non-fiction:
How the Italians Created Canada
In the Name of Hockey

A Jar
of Fireflies

Josie Di Sciascio-Andrews

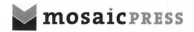

Library and Archives Canada Cataloguing in Publication

Title: A jar of fireflies / Josie Di Sciascio-Andrews.

Names: Di Sciascio-Andrews, Josie, 1955- author.

Description: Poems | Previously published in 2015.

Identifiers: Canadiana (print) 20240281314
                Canadiana (ebook) 20240281322

ISBN 9781771617444 (softcover) ISBN 9781771617451 (PDF)
ISBN 9781771617468 (EPUB) ISBN 9781771617475 (Kindle)

Subjects: LCGFT: Poetry.
Classification: LCC PS8607.I73 J37 2024 | DDC C811/.6—dc23

Published by Mosaic Press, Oakville, Ontario, Canada, 2024.
MOSAIC PRESS, Publishers
www.Mosaic-Press.com
Copyright © Josie Di Sciascio-Andrews, 2024

Printed and bound in Canada.

ONTARIO ARTS COUNCIL
CONSEIL DES ARTS DE L'ONTARIO
an Ontario government agency
un organisme du gouvernement de l'Ontario

ONTARIO CREATES

Funded by the Government of Canada
Financé par le gouvernement du Canada | Canadä

MOSAIC PRESS
1252 Speers Road, Units 1 & 2, Oakville, Ontario, L6L 5N9 (905) 825-2130
info@mosaic-press.com • www.mosaic-press.com

Memories light up the landscapes of our nights like fireflies:
places, loves, children, friends lighting up our lives
to defy despair. Small tinder sticks of hope.
Little miracles twinkling in the dark.

For Ryan and Matthew

Contents

Sea Glass

a few good memories
scattered in the sands of time
magical glass blinking sunlight
broken pieces of emerald and aquamarine blue
I pick you up
the treasures of a child's heart
my heart
forever searching
on the beaches of my younger days
the Adriatic Sea
when my father drove us there
and the world was whole
when the crash of the waves against the shore
was most immense to the senses
like the sound of the universe
the sound of God
white foam receding
scattering seashells and other treasures
in the wet sand
pieces of life
boiled up from the depths of the ocean
sea glass
broken pieces
more beautiful now
than the original object
they once formed
a menial bottle
a utility jar
now a jewel
because of its brokenness
polished
by the incessant waves
of time
the transmuter
of all things

Josie Di Sciascio-Andrews

Unus Mundus

when everything fails
there's always memory

imagination frees me
from reality's shackles
and I plunge
through wormholes of time
to my childhood world
that enchanted place within

untainted oceans
forever blue skies
expanding universe
on the rainbow gossamer
of soap bubbles
my young life
a new breath
before the winds of destiny
carried it away
to faraway worlds
before wholeness splintered
into a thousand selves

see me here
now
my seeming wisdom

enter my eyes
sidestep the shattered glass
in my heart

take my hand
back in time
and I will show you paradise
at the bottom of the well

A Jar of Fireflies

I will always remember
My mother on an August night,
As if every other moment before
Or after, had coalesced into one
Giant memory of her.
Crux of all maternal symbology.
Moon and stars leavening
In the indigo belly of summer.
A fecundity of fireflies fluttering invisible
Flurries of wings, glowed a soft, slow magic.
Caught glints of her earrings
Amidst black curls falling
Upon her Renoir-print
Green flowered dress.
In the growing shadows
She told me things. I listened.
Watching her every move,
As she watered geranium
And basil in brick-edged
Garden beds. Petals
Pungent of earth.
Scent galvanizing
Time and space. Proust-like.
Involuntary.
Etching the wonder of the two of us,
As we stood in some primordial paradise,
While all around, a universe of galactic stardust
Revolved. Enveloping us. And from the microcosm,
New, like undiscovered dreams,
Thousands of fireflies promised illusions
Of ageless never nevers.
She was my planet. I was her small moon.
Together in our little garden, snug as the snails.
Safely at a distance from both birth and death,
For one eternal moment, we stood certain
Upon that soil of lettuces and pale petunias,
While far off, the streets buzzed

With their cacophony of cars and voices.
Up close, behind the laurel leaves, a scarab
Tucked away its iridescent wing. And the fig tree
Curled a webbed leaf around its purple fruit.
My mother's shadow held me close too.
Like a hushing. A silent belonging to the earth.
To the blood that bore us. Like everything
And everyone before and after.
The earth holding us up like a new crop
For a seemingly endless season.

Sunflower Dream

I stood alone in a dream
My back to copper rays of light
Folding behind shadowed hills
Under the racing clouds of a darkening sky.

Behind me, forever fields of sunflowers
Swayed the benevolent faces of a million sun gods.

Black seeds encircled with yellow petal coronas.
Warm, sensual life auras
Calling me back from darkness.

My gaze lost for too long in the crystal ball of a divining sky.
My body, a dot on the never ending road of another country.

In Nonna's House

these are the roses
I picked in nonna's garden

these are the peaches

here is the bottle
I filled in her wine cellar

here is the carafe of olive oil

scattered on the blue tablecloth
are the books I have read

half a dozen spilled fruits

sunlight is splashing
on a framed purple sea
hanging on a yellow wall

beyond
a dog sleeps in the corner
ear twitching at a fly

the tap is leaking

summer breeze fills the curtain
with cicadas' circular echoes

I am but a point in space
standing
in concentric circles of memory

all those places
all those loved ones

alive
at the centre
of this still life

Josie Di Sciascio-Andrews

Flowers in Blue Vase

this blue clay vase
so rough to the touch

beneath my fingertips
the leaves are velvet tongues

still life of zinnias,
daffodils and marigolds
arrange the view
on blue linen tablecloth

outside
behind the window pane
dreamscapes glisten

the earth bequests
beyond the cultivated fields
to chance our way
through groves of thickest darkness

see the empty barn
its dark blind eye

see the fields of nettles
bloodying the purple hills,
crowning them with silver clouds

between these blooms
and that far away light
the years ripple

back to the centre
pieces on another table

in another time
of another place
we once called home

Josie Di Sciascio-Andrews

Geraniums on a Patio in Positano

What is it about the colour red
That draws me in?

Like blood calling blood

As if the rest did not exist:
The softest hues of dovetail grey
Blurring into white cloud and rock.

Pale blue skies dripping like tears.
Washing over the muted fibres
Of verdigris landscapes.

Sadness seeping deeper
In the growing emptiness
Of time slipping past.

Red instead rekindles
The eye's gaze
To flirt with the sun.

Blushing the cheeks
Of ripening fruit

In a country
I could fall in love with
For its joyful feast of summer.
Where geranium petals
Cascade from balconies.

Bloom red
Like the hearts
Of women sitting
Behind old glass panes.

Stoking hope like embers
To outlive the fog's paleness.

Josie Di Sciascio-Andrews

The Red Accordion

By ear, at five
My father learned to play
An instrument too big
For tiny shoulders to endure.
On slow, hot afternoons
After a day of harvest,
Zio Domenico offered him wine,
Secrets of manhood, cigarettes.
Strapped an accordion
To his tender arms
Then taught his little fingers
To seek out harmonic nuances
On a pearly keyboard to the right,
While cohering rhythm from the randomness
Of small, black buttons to the left.
Two ventricles
Bellowing in and out the sound
Waves of a universe expanding
From a silken, fanned out lung
Opening wide the landscape of a life.
Inevitably returning
To the corpus callosum of itself
Collapsing beauty shut.
Like a butterfly with pleated paper wings
My father mastered syncopated rhapsodies
Moulding heart to calculated sequences.
Keeping tempo
In the gaps.
Like heart beats.
Time in one hand,
Space in the other.
A tiny God
Juggling spheres.

Josie Di Sciascio-Andrews

I always remember him middle-aged.
Sitting on the basement couch
Of the Oakville bungalow
He bought for us in 1970.
I still see him with a glass
Of whisky or home-made wine
Before a winter night
Shift at the refinery. Teary-eyed
And nostalgic. Playing old tunes
On a second-hand accordion.
I remember how it bothered him.
Unable to reach a certain note
Because of a missing key.
He had his eye on a new, red one
That he'd seen in a music shop window
in Clarkson - was planning to buy it
After the last mortgage payment
Of what was to become his last spring.
On the broken accordion
The sound was good regardless.
How like my father to make good
Of the worst and the mediocre.
His fingers harmonizing joy
For us, in allegro, andante.
Improvising the frenzied flights
Of old world soundscapes.
Waltzes and tangos. Mazurkas.
Inevitably entering into the segues of silence.
The long, slow notes of a loveless winter.
And then briefly, the joyful reprieve
Of a ripresa stitching back
The sweetness of a lyrical refrain
From some top-forty radio hit
Like "Tie a Yellow Ribbon
'Round the Old Oak Tree".

A heart zigzagging spasmodic
Sound right to the end.

Like a blood song.

A song beginning.
A song ending.
With so much urgent striving in between.

Sicily

She is the lover you couldn't tame.
Scylla and Charybdis' dangerous lure.

Her golden skin, a land of sun and temples.
Of lemon groves. Of cactus.

Homer's odyssey of Magna Graecia.
Rome's coveted pearl.

Blessed by Africa since birth
With zephyrs and scirocco winds
Dusting her waves from the Sahara.

Precious child of Carthage and Troy.
Cupid's Psyche, taken with force
By blue-eyed Normandy.

She is the woman you had to leave behind.
The poverty a man must overcome
In order to survive.

That void in the heart
You have tried in vain to fill
With new-found worldly pleasures.
Things to replace her.

She is your deep-seated longing.
Your mother, country, missing half.
Mediterranean Eve.

A golden pyramid.

Antony's Cleopatra
Undaunted by fate.

Alone
Against her bitter history

Of barbarous conquests,
Pillagings, criminal sons.

Medusa's Gorgon lair
Of unexpected dangers
Rising from her deep, dark seas.
Screaming in silent outrage.

From Messina to Siracusa
Under turquoise Aegean skies,
Trinacria bares her sun-kissed landscape.

Throws back her tropical mane.
Unveils her Muslim mosques.
Sheds centuries of black Madonna garments.

Etna cries out her passion.

At dusk, Sicilia chants her ancient vespers.
Whispers her Latin mantras
On strings of worn rosary beads
Chaining her to ever changing lovers,
Masters, Gods.
Terra Patris.

And you will think of her often.
Dream of her.
Long for her bittersweet embrace.
Dolce amaro.
Like an almond
Searching for its shell.
A child seeking roots.
Your tabernacle. Holy cusp.

And even though you haven't been with her
For a thousand years,
You will carry her in your heart
Like a genetic memory
Of blood, of family, of race.

Josie Di Sciascio-Andrews

She is your land.
Your soil.
Though you may walk a million miles from her
On the frozen tundras of another continent,
You will not be able to shake her.

The darkness of her waves
In your own hair.

The olive tinge of her hills
In the hues of your own skin.

Her almond trees blossoming
In the telltale shape of your eyes.

And again, you will love her.

Move to her rhythms
In the hypnotic trance of an Ozark harp.
The wild unshackling of Turkish tambourines.
The unexpected thump,
Guttural human hum.
Determined heel step. Knuckle drum.
The strum of blood throbbing at the nape
For one poisonous tarantula's kill.
Survival dance.

Despite time.
Despite the distance,
Her magic will lure you back
And once again you will succumb
To her hypnotic guiles
For you will recognize in her
Yourself.

My Father's House

Poplars' silver leaves chime their silent song
Unchaining themselves to hot wind
Blowing north from Africa.
Powdering red dust on the blue river
Where my father fished when he was a boy.

Those were the days of magical hills
Beyond which, mythical forefathers cast spells on memory.

Dark moustached heroes with old fashioned names
Commanding awe beside crucifixes
In yellowed portraits on the whitewashed walls
Of my father's house.

Grapes still hang from sunlit foliaged vines
Covering the old cobblestones with green patterned light.

Wheat fields sway their rugged tresses
And unkempt rose gardens spill their fragrant bloom
On the weathered river cane fences
My grandfather built.

Near the old stone barn, a rope swing hangs
From a gnarled fig tree.
Forgotten.

Everyone has died. Gone
To the city or America.

Once, when my father was young
Heaven was here.

Before the war.
Before the world aged.

When a lull of seeming serenity
Embraced time.

Josie Di Sciascio-Andrews

Memories

I like telephone poles

there's a row of them in my back yard
black wires disappearing through pines
back in time along some imaginary trajectory

sunlight breaking on the sea's horizon
large golden waves rolling in on the Adriatic
along stretches of sand and stones
speckled with colourful beach umbrellas

a train speeds out of a mountain tunnel
weaving through poplars and olive groves
around the blonde hills of wheat and oleander

below church towers and terracotta rooftops
appearing and disappearing in sunlight

these are the stitched up photographs
of places I carry in my soul

Mediterranean blue skies
transcending time and space

when I look out the window, telephone poles
always lead me back along the wires

to my first encounter with the ocean
the hometown in my heart

when I was young
and the world was raw sensation
like the first impact with Eden

back when everything was joy
and every fruit was mine for the taking

Creation

Out of nothing
I have created love.

Silver webs of light
in endless days.

Memories shining
bright in photographs
of my children's play on sunny beaches.
Old willow trees turned pirate ship.
Fishing on Bronte Pier.

It breaks me up
to reminisce
my children.
Their young voices calling me
in videos.
Now that they're men.
Now that they push me away
in search of masculine autonomy.
I understand.
I know it's right
and yet,
I long for their cherub faces
sleepy after a bath in soft flannel pyjamas,
begging for one more bedtime story.

It chokes me up, this lack of them
the way they used to be.

This time passing,
trampling on our sand castles
blowing out
yet another birthday cake of candles.
Another year
into a strange tomorrow.

Josie Di Sciascio-Andrews

Heart

behind a poem's written lines
lies a heart, open
cut and bleeding, unseen
behind the bleached paper
writhing painfully on a sterile page
it wants to scream, but it has no mouth
it wants to run, but it has no legs
it is a heart beating wildly
without a brain, it can't be taken seriously
it can't be trusted
a heart dying
in a printer
wired to spill out onto the whiteness of a page
stylized pain

what is the truth behind the lines?
is it an S.O.S. from the heart?
is it emotion spilling out
through the walls of convention?
climbing out from the barbed wire
of my civilized mind?

a message
from the heart
behind the ink
behind the lines
behind the paper
behind ...

... a secret path within
to the darkness
to the relegated memories
in the realms of my mind
to the place I saw behind the black gate
in the dark alley
where the old woman sits and knits
inside the dark door behind her

Josie Di Sciascio-Andrews

upstairs
in a warm room
where love sleeps
and dreams

Watermelon Memories

summer days split open
like slices of ripe watermelon

crisp, red, juicy flesh
frosted with sweetness

how we dug into them,
relished in the freshness
of those humble moments

I have a photograph of us
after a watermelon feast
two neighbours, my mother and I
standing beside a white Vespa

from our ages and what we are wearing
it must have been 1963
my sister unborn in my mother's belly
my father out of view behind the camera
"watermelon is like the Italian flag"
he always said, "green, white and red"
"except for the black pits" I always thought
"but perhaps because of them" I later learned

already so much nostalgia for a country
we hadn't left yet, premonitions
of summer days that would end
fall like dark watermelon seeds
into foreign soil, where we would lose
ourselves, growing new tendrils
forever doomed to recreate
those first protean moments
elsewhere, like all first loves
the memory of them superimposed
upon all future loves, indelible
scars burned like sun blasts
in the canyons of the heart

Josie Di Sciascio-Andrews

Migrations

they come back
repeat like the call of a drum
those moments that marked my time

like murdered Gods
in white shrouds of history

always there
waiting to be resurrected
behind the heavy stone
of reason's portals

corpses like Jesus, like holy ghosts
my divine trinities

me in love at twenty one
with you forever
telling me that I'm beautiful

nonna waving goodbye
at her door for the last time

my father's final words
from a hospital room stretcher
bloodied with the urgency
of a ruptured heart
a broken dream

my family on an emigrant ship
four demoted kings and queens
bereft of crowns and constellations

a ship's glass door lifting up
like the globe of a compass
revealing the direction of death's alternative

Josie Di Sciascio-Andrews

a ladder and rescue boat below
wavering needles in the darkest centre of the Atlantic

a country left behind, a bluer sky
a mother tongue, a civilization

piazzas like the dark pupils of familiar eyes
their hazel streets at dusk, the strands of an iris
golden around the lens of things

black centre points of all future cohesion
from which everything else would spawn

from the tiniest remembered things

like atoms of the long gone
dust of all that matters

The Hidden City

Zooming in
up close,
the postcard memory
of a place
disappears.
With magnification
the edges fade,
as asphalt, brick and skin
expose their microscopic
infinities.
Panning out,
everything reverts
back to incognito delineations
of grey, concrete architecture.
The city floats
on a flat line of perception.
High and low rises accrue
solidity like stalagmites.
Below their cellared caves,
in humid undergrounds,
commuters inch their way
through revolving doors,
down metal escalators
to the netherworld
of subway tunnels.
Depending on who we are
or where we stand, human
accampments are mutable.
Like everything else
we see with the naked eye,
they unfold, beyond a myriad buildings
and facades, their many hidden secrets.
Because like a love affair,
a city is what we take with us.
What we keep.
The snapshot of a street.
The aerial view of skyscrapers

Josie Di Sciascio-Andrews

in traffic congested avenues
neglect a million stories.
Like clouds, millions of passersby
forever glance at their reflections
in glass mirrored windows.
The unexpected garden
always surprises
behind the mask
of wall, like a pupil
of labyrinthine dimensions
behind the dullness of a closed lid.
And one can always digress
away from the linear,
geometrical order mortared
upon the wilderness.
Beyond a maze
of offices and condos,
the sudden glimpse of teal waves
arouses the blood
to rush unabated
to breathe in the lake's raw throb
like a child running towards home's open door
or a lover to an unobstructed kiss.
As if God, or everything
were indeed inside the eye of a needle,
mesmerizing our gaze unto itself
in the guise of water and sky;
in the treasure of unkempt weedy patches
thriving their unstructured possibilities
in the secrecy of an unseen alley;
peering from the manic stare of a beggar.
The apple tree again,
offering forever fruits of paradise
from the confines of a man made atrium
like a warm feathered sparrow;
a heart beating
from the unlatched door
of a cage of ribs.

Josie Di Sciascio-Andrews

"One day you will understand me," my father said.

Inside the whale
You wait for me.

With your ancient wine.
Your smouldering candle.

Ageless.

You sit in the dark corner
Of an epiglottis.

Dead. Yet undead.
Suspended in memory.

I have drowned.

Around my neck
A rope of heavy stones
Has snuffed out all illusion.

Scourged
I have arrived
At your small altar
Of sacrifice.

Your shoulders are bent
Father.

In your eyes burns a humble wisdom.
Of the world that fails.

The ominous world
Of blind cats and lame foxes.

All false fire eaters.

The ocean's gaping mouth,
Maw of all things,
Like time
Has taken us.

I am here to drink
Of your cup.

Your eyes are tiny points of light
Guiding me back
From the cave
Of all unraveling.

Premonition

The wind is coming
my darling.

The gusts will arrive
unexpectedly.

Like those express trains
from exotic places,

rushing out of dark tunnels,

then braking hastily
with premonitions
of love and happiness.

The wind is coming
my love.

It will blow dust,
newspaper pages

in the odd, oblique light
of unsettling dreams,

cutting geometrical shadows
against the glow
of bare city streets.

It will toss
in the mad dance of branches

bending signs
and certainties.

With winter's skeletal fingers
it will rap its' ghostly bones
at our windowpanes

Josie Di Sciascio-Andrews

startling us
from the trance of sleep.

It will bend the oleander bloom.
Disperse its scent
of pungent newness,

dishevel ivy's long tendrils
from wrought-iron balconies.

The wind is coming
my darling.

You will hear its' growing clap
echoing
in the mad frenzy of chimes.

It will tame the anger.

Soften the spunk
of new skin's turgor.

Release illusions.

Undo all reason,
making of hope
a weary promise.

It will toss belief
into a fitful sleep
urging us to surrender

to the heavy quilt
of mystery

strewn like debris
of time
across our hearts

asking us only in return
for our quiescence.

Poetic Alchemy

I spin golden words from my world of straw.
I extrapolate wonder from the commonplace.

The centre is anywhere I am.

For there is no other place.
No other happiness
Other than the piece of sky
I expand with my yearning.

My eyes create reality
With the poetic palette of blood hues:
The deep reds, the melancholy blues.

I strike a match on stone
And memory ignites it to diamond.

I immortalize people and places
I have loved.

The real world pales
While within me,

The universe explodes
With the infinite

Colours of creation.

Reverie

Alone with pen and paper
I am a poet.

Mind poised to merge
With the ineffable whisper
Of the mysterious
In everyday things.

I am every woman.
Every man
That ever came before.
That ever will be.

I am mind reaching
Through the periphery
Of my senses. Veering
Into land and sky.
Neither hunting, nor harvesting.

My thoughts caress landscapes
Like strong, gentle winds.
Brushing out tall, dead grasses
Into endless fields of memories.

Alone with pen and paper
I am a web of strings and feathers.

A dream catcher.
Sitting on the tip of a crescent moon.

I cast silver lines into the darkness.
Reeling in the ghosts of a diaphanous past.

Josie Di Sciascio-Andrews

The Poem

perhaps the poem
is what we could never grasp

the ethereal gap
between brain synapses

of what was almost ours
for a fleeting moment

memories of happiness
once had
sting with the blade
of murdered hope

how steep
was the sudden fall
when the summit had been reached

words sculpt life's meaning
into statues

encrypt stones
with weathered, mossy epitaphs

perhaps the poem
is what composes randomness

the weave that spins chaos
into coherent thought

words ribboning
bunches of memories

like wild flowers
tied with humble string

Josie Di Sciascio-Andrews

nostalgia bleeds
with the ache of loss

and the words
spill out simply

This Poem

what can this poem bring
that you don't already know?

everything already said

the same old words
budding new leaves
of ancient wisdom

the quintessential
reappearing
in new configurations

segments of eternity
encapsulated
within a crystal
of burgeoning hope
for you to hold

this glimpse of life
stylized in ink

pulled
from the mind's circuitry

infinitesimal fragments
of light, shards

of the broken mirror
of the absolute

reflecting flares of sun
their intense mercurial fire

flashing
from the tiniest splinters

Josie Di Sciascio-Andrews

Raison d'Etre

this is the urgent poem

voice
giving
birth
to the child
heart
animal caged
escaping

human
without haloes
without wings

visceral, primal call
of death destined Eros
suddenly aware
of Eden's long told lie

mind's frantic computation
of the body's tawdry wrestle
with time

Woman Sitting at Bus Stop

I saw her sitting
On a bench
At Third Line and Lakeshore.
Hair white as a scarecrow.
That's when it hit
Like cold wind.
Autumn leaves, snowflakes
Falling upon her
In the midst of spring.
Her vacant eyes transfixed
On faraway clock towers.
Hands clasping a purse
Of memories. Better days
Ticking on her wrist watch
Reflecting clouds
At the speed of time.
I saw her sitting silently,
Still as a statue.
Her life played out
from a to z.
That's when it hit
Like a celluloid dream.
Life fast forwarded.
Rewound.
She could be me.
And soon
She would be gone.

The Circus of Night Dreams

Against blue darkness
tall pines
etch ominous crystals
in the cave of night.

Their inverted roots
burrowing deep shadows
in vast emptiness.

North star, a pin
firm in its' place
holds up the night
like a circus tent
above our town.

I stand
on a velvet fold of karma.
All unuttered thoughts
bouncing back
to their own source of gravity.
Such agile gymnasts
elastic on their trampolines.
Trapeze artists skimming tightropes.
Elephants, tigers
braving hoops of deathly flames.
Parades of human talent,
beauties, frightening beasts
flaunting their tamed, glittered ferocities.
Each gift, each oddity
of the whole gawdy world
dangling
from ropes in midair
as an audience forever gasps
to the unexpected drum roll.
We, the acrobats
with our telltale garb.
Our own bejewelled limbs flailing,

Josie Di Sciascio-Andrews

leaping towards other hands,
blindly seeking.
Grasping at solid objects
in the ever growing possibility
of falling
without nets.

The Moon

I am the moon
round
distant
cold light
reflecting the sun's warmth
back to a blue planet
a lover's smile
forever light years away
black space
gravity pulling tidal waves
of emotion
forever love
on shores of childhood dreams

I am the moon
pale maiden in the morning sky
large orange crone at dusk
alone
I ignite the dark
for moonlight kisses

Josie Di Sciascio-Andrews

Love

look at me
like you would look at the lake

tenderness rising up like a tide
in the midst of your everyday
thoughts of me

I want to remember you
like this

eyes
deep as the ocean

silences
dripping with sentiment

your heart and mine
crashing
within the same wave

Of Love and Writing

you cannot force the poem

it comes when it will
on butterfly wings of kismet

sails whole with wind
blowing along deep blue oceans
hide their reasoned intricacies
beneath reality's perfect skin

words too, they pull
mind, heart, senses
to shared images of worlds
we all have known

like the dark green brush strokes
of weather bent pines
cutting against wisps of white
in cool blue northern skies

the evenings spent casting lines
in ponds of golden sunsets

while longings took flight
in the cries of the night owl

no, you cannot force the poem

it comes when it will
in the softness of a lover's face

with lips of promise
it will lure you
to unknown labyrinths
where mind meets mind

Josie Di Sciascio-Andrews

where heart's door unlatches
to the blissful, dangerous rush
of limitless space

A Cardinal in the Cedars

A cardinal in the cedars
Is such a wonderful thing.

A dash of red
Amidst drab, winter foliage.

Life calling out
With unabashed boldness,

As if to spite the marbled tomb
Of cold, nebulous skies.

A glimpse of fleeting passion.
Short lived, fearful lover's lust.

So bold. So true.
So swiftly gone.

Your Eyes

your eyes
light up my heart
set ablaze sunsets
beyond the dance of bare branches
in cold January wind

your eyes ribbon my sky
with streams of light
mirroring clouds of blue Mondays
on beveled panes of gothic windows

your eyes
ensnare, lasso
those parts of me I had caged
forgotten
beneath veneers of nonchalance

your perfect words
this empty heart
roped in
by threads of incandescence
tying knots and bows
with my veins
like gifts

Josie Di Sciascio-Andrews

Your Voice

Your voice is a loon
On the lake at dawn
Calling my name
Between waves of wakefulness and dreams
Red fire breaking on grey skylines
With promises of sunrise
On dark horizons

Josie Di Sciascio-Andrews

Tsunami

you are tsunami in my heart
black wave at high sea
unexpected danger .

your eyes
so dark, so deep
submerging will
eyes to drown in

you are tsunami in my soul
quake unannounced
in the harbour of my days

star lover
ocean gazer
my kindred passion
you

Love's Treasure

This night is a pirate
With its scarf of stars.

Its earring moon.

Blue ink seagulls tattooed
On the flexing arm of an Indian sky.

Dreams take sail on milky blue seas
With the white shirt frills of curling waves
Spilling their lacy foam on belts of sand
On the washed out grey of old driftwood stumps.

Tonight a creaking ghost ship sails.
Love is the captain.
A pirate hidden behind the open canvas.

By the lighthouse
Beyond the fog,
A maiden waits.

Yes, and there's treasure too
In dusty trunks
Of ancient maps marked with crosses.
Worms burrowing in the empty eye sockets
Of yellowed skulls.
Hooks instead of hands.
Half burned candles.
Empty bottles of rum.
And so the story goes
Of a maiden, a pirate,
A carved out heart
Doomed to haunt the waves
Searching for missed treasure.

Lovers and stars
Like buried coins
In the chest of night.

Josie Di Sciascio-Andrews

Dangerous Reflection

I am the ghost of a dove.

Invisible trembling of wind
Through the branches of trees
Bare in the throes of winter.

Did you hear the sudden thud
At your window pane?

Did you see me hit?
Did you look away?

It was so unexpected
This falling.

Having mistaken sky
In the solid reflection
Of your soul exposed
Like sun and clouds
Behind a cold, glass eye.

Winter Love

a wedge of lemon
moon
hangs on the rim
of night

this night
cold, winter blue
studded with distant stars

while I hold your gaze
in my heart
warm, like a sun

I defend you
within me

against cold's anger
rational, icy chill

the shiver
of this winter light

reflecting loveless shadows
on the diamond skin of snow

Josie Di Sciascio-Andrews

Memories of you on Karl Johan Street

Poem inspired by Marlene Bird's Surrealist Pillow—the painting behind
the woman sitting on the couch is Edvard Munch's "Evening on Karl Johan
Street"

I pretended not to see you Edvard
on that cold winter evening,
as you walked alone
towards the bruised darkness.

I would have run to you,
had I not been with him
walking on the other side
following the homebound crowd.

I knew it was you.
Your profile,
The hologram
Of love forever imprinted
On my heart.

Now I sit on the sofa
Of Charon's vestibule
forever knitting my way back.

Behind me hangs the dream of you.
We are converging lines
on one point in time
for eternity
away from sunlight.

I have saved bottles of time.
Precious sea glass in sand
as the centre pieces of my life.

A thousand years of purple pills
will grant me sleep,
though you will not return
to wake me.

Josie Di Sciascio-Andrews

I have poisoned my own apple, Edvard.
Cast myself out of heaven.
Bloodied my own innocence
With the serpent's words.
The lure of so many reasons.

Josie Di Sciascio-Andrews

Vitruvian Heartbreak

When a heart shatters
What bargain does it make?

What fixed point .
Of which rigid axis
Does it nail itself to
In order to avoid the angst
Of further incohesion?

One must not underestimate
The consequence of error.

A snag in time alters
The ocean's current.
Curves the hands of clocks.
Breaks symmetries.

Whatever lead you
To eschew my love
Must have had its reasons.

My appetite for truth.
Your laconic answers
Left me no respite
From the fire of regret.

I delved into the centre
Of your every word.
Blind, centrifugal digger.
A mole burrowing
In tunnels of meaning
For flickering clues of love.
Spinning in circles
Like a mad gyroscope.
Crucified to the pivotal darkness.

Ghost

Tonight the fog
Hastens towards our headlights.

The absence of things
Glaring through the mist.

The thick of it.

Where road and curb erase
What's left of tree trunks.

Torsos of bark
Dispersed
In diaphanous veils.

In the silence,
A heart beats still.

Innocent.
Wide eyed.

Like a deer
Struck in the glare
Of oncoming traffic.

Just another casualty
Too unimportant to report.

Josie Di Sciascio-Andrews

Landscape

Why do I feel most at home
On a day like this
When after a night of heavy rain
Light smudges morning
Onto the hard edges of things.
It makes me want to ponder
Mystical philosophies
Of inner and outer worlds.
Me absorbing nature
Within the porous skin
Of my poetic soul.
The whole of sky
Fluting out of myself
Like an extension
Of my brain with its pale
Aura of clouds folding coils
Of meaning into the grooves
Of my own grey matter.
On this foggy morning
The chrome-yellow centre line
Painted on the wet asphalt
Unfurls networks of neuronal highways
Intersecting through old, familiar
Yet forever changing channels of memories.
Like my own closed fists
The trees are holding onto their buds
Tightly in this precarious weather.
Reticent to yield their essence
As they wait for the benevolent warmth
Of the sun to relent their bloom
Willingly. Reveal their full dendritic growth
Spilling clusters of flowers
Their pastel hues finally softening
The angular harshness of concrete objects
With heavy snowfalls of petals.
On a morning like this
Everything is on the verge

Josie Di Sciascio-Andrews

Of becoming.
Behind the veil of fog
Everything exists at once, somewhere
In this landscape of the visible,
The unseen, the erased.
Bombs exploding out of sight
Somewhere in the synapses
Are muffled by magnolias
Blooming pink like dopamine.
Beyond the sunny conflagrations
Of forsythia, tragedies too, recede.
Out of the mist, the sense of things
Emerges like an arm with a sword
From a cold, grey lake.
My own pale hand holding the metal
Wand, retrieved from a stony prison
Where, with the precise eye
Of a sculptor, I have learned to chisel
Catastrophes and chimeras
Into marble gods.

Sunrise Over Lake Ontario

white seagulls perch
on grey driftwood
on beaches of sand and stones
early in the morning
when the orange sun
rises majestic over Lake Ontario
hugging the planet with fire
blowing light
across blue waves
filling my eyes with happiness

welcome gift
this vermilion warmth
I seek all year

this summer gladness
that takes me back
to all the sunrises of my life
before heartbreak
before the fall in darkened skies
when scenes like this were enough
my heart in a diorama
the earth's colours and mine
one

Lightning Over the Lake

this is a night of storms
splintering against window panes

the kind that swells evening waves
surprising us with moonless dark

this is a night of storms
rage of high winds

tormented sleep, howling lake
and trees, merging reality with dreams

fear's cold hands on my shoulders
lightning cracking at the window

this house or another
love here or gone

Pigeons

he called me
and another poem died
while I was writing,
trying to catch the flow
of my ideas
before they vanished

and fly away they did
spooked
like pigeons
in a piazza
bursting away in the sky
at a stark sound
cutting
through
the fractal waves
of my imaginings
demanding something
reminding me to come back
to the real
pretend
to stop being
the daydreamer
I really am

Josie Di Sciascio-Andrews

Reflection

I have mulled this world over
for so long
it has become me
an extension of me

waves of steely blue lake
like blood flow, ebbing
from arteries to veins
in invisible rhythm
sky breathing air
in lungs, branches

pain and beauty
folded in with flowers, sunsets
fear and love of death
in one view

this immense blue water and sky
tears and laughter
me
in the world

Josie Di Sciascio-Andrews

Summer Dreams

Oakville pier
disappears in fog
on hot muggy mornings
lake and sky blending in grey mist

on the wharf, the lighthouse
beckons the eye
red stripe on white
beyond mounds of wild grass
blue chicory
silver lace

along the Sixteenth Mile's murky waters
sailboats' tall masts sway
hypnotic
"Scarab", "Dreamin", Ulysses"
names for adventure
hulls to sail away on
at high seas
away from torpid waters
into blue oceans
new worlds
the sun

Between Here and Somewhere

before nightfall
the sun sets on the darkening earth
radiating the glow of red light spectrum

bare branches
etch black ink capillaries
against a northern sky

the last of the geese honk
their farewell
announcing impending snow storms

this is the frame of a captured moment
the stillness of a realization

between here and somewhere
I have felt warmth

between here and somewhere
I have loved

Josie Di Sciascio-Andrews

Winter Musings

Geese fly in formation towards a pale sun.
The lake is blue slate, warmed by tenuous strokes of
     copper light.
Wind calls through dark, skeletal trees.

Is it the cry of love lost long ago?
Is it the voice of love lost yesterday?

Maybe it's the abysmal need for my father's reassuring
     presence.
Wind howling my soul's longing for that which seemed to be.
For that which will never come again, yet returns endlessly
In the echo of wind and waves.

The last of the frozen oak leaves festoon their old age
Clinging to branches like obsessive lovers.
Pretending to belong, when they have long been jilted.

They too will fall, like everything else.
There is no mercy for that which has had its day.

Endless Winter

It snowed again today
On the first day of spring.

Thick, white snowflakes
On branches instead of blossoms.

An enchanted world.
Black and white silent stillness.

Snow falling steadily.
Forever it seems, this year
Like a depression that never lifts.

White sky, like the eye of a blind man
Staring out at nothingness
Refracting an internal gaze
On his long lost memories
Of colours and love
Hoping for some repeat performance.

Like me, shivering behind the window.
Hoping it will be spring tomorrow.

Forecast

On cool, fall mornings
Large white clouds mushroom
Like mounds of snow
Over Lake Ontario
Reminding us
Of impending winter.

And it's the wind that speaks.
Its' voice a chill
Of frozen skies to come.
Of ice already had.

Endless stretches of sterility.
Consciousness clinging
To memories of summer.

Life's delusions glorified
in the mind's recasting.

Our life slipping away
As we fend off
Another season of ice storms.

Inspired by Ovid's Metamorphoses

one wave
one gust of wind
again, love, you emerge
out of a dream
through the invisible glass of air
conceal your form in trees
the intricate landscape
of leaves and clouds
a sparrow's form camouflaged
in feathered, warm blood
tethering its' tiny movements
to the earth

again, a winter sky
transfixes its' blue gaze
upon my hair

bare branches
netted up against memory

the faded pearl of sun
brushing evanescence
against the salt parched roads
and frozen January grasses
scourged by unrelenting winds

defiant hearts colliding
everywhere like air fronts

Josie Di Sciascio-Andrews

All that glitters

All that glitters
calls me to itself.

Incessant is the lure of sparkles
on frozen January roads
beaming their frost
in the morning sun
like teeth
in the mouth of the world.

I am a crow
stirred by tinsel
and city lights
ringing their chimes
of false happiness
like aircraft
I mistook for stars
on dark, lonely nights.

I have been searching
for the flame that pulls me.
Sun, moon, starlight.
Crumbs of comforting bread
To guide my lost heart
home.

Josie Di Sciascio-Andrews

"And yet, there is only one great thing; the only thing: to live, to see, in
huts and on journeys,the great day that dawns and the light that fills the
world." (Inuit Song)

River of Light

"a living light shone round me, leaving me bathed in such a
        veil of its brightness,
that nothing was visible to me. 'The Love, that stills Heaven,
        always accepts spirits, into itself,
with such a greeting, to fit the candle for its flame.... and I
        saw brightness, in the form of a river,
shining, amber, between banks pricked out with miraculous
        spring. Living sparks flashed from this river,
and fell into the blossoms on all sides, like gold-set rubies.
        Then they plunged themselves, again,
into the marvellous vortex, as if drunk with the perfumes,
        and as one entered, another issued out.
Sun spoke to me, then added: 'The river and the topazes that
        enter it and exit, and the smile of the grasses,
are the shadowy preface to their reality. Not because the
        things are crude in themselves, but the defect is in you,
because you do not have such exalted vision yet."

Paradiso, Dante

Josie Di Sciascio-Andrews

Renewal

at dawn, sunlight
pours down again
through the sky's membrane
colouring the world
with the pale hues
of glass marbles

renewal
rolls down from the ether
unfolding kaleidoscopic magic
in the eyes of a new day
young again
reborn
in the seeming stasis
of earth

forever new
blooming
with the quintessential
lure of a young woman
babies' angel hair flowing
in spring breezes

morning light
of our own soul
renewing itself
while marbles of the past spin
away from our fingers
into the hands of children
weaving new trajectories
in the relentless game of destiny
where space and time intersect
to recreate the world

Spring Morning

the dandelions have returned
like a million little suns

such childish diadems
bursting yellow rays of joy
on the dark fringed brow
of green May grasses
fragrant with the hope
of seemingly empty space

dark matter teeming
with possibilities of renewal

soon, their thin petal strips will fall
like short lived loves
their orgasmic sunbursts
replaced with downy puffs of seed

haloes of a million tiny candles
each homely flame, an arrow

sharp, like truths behind all pleasures
like children waiting to be born

beyond the falling stars of lust
burned off sparklers
extinguished suns

exchanging macroscopic incandescence
for the small smolderings
of bloomlessness

the uneventful life of ordinary days
left over in spades
of bitter foliage

Josie Di Sciascio-Andrews

after the brief bright joys
the memory of them
redeeming the rest
of the mundane existence
of the beautiless
rooted in the humble earth

The Earth Laughs in Flowers*

Ralph Waldo Emerson

Sometimes, the poem arrives
like a love song on a summer morning.
Soft notes caught in mid-air.

Tuned to the inward hum
of its rhythmic cadence,
we lean into the light
no wiser than the daffodils.

With that same naive eagerness
of crocuses, we extricate ourselves
out of the darkness to be born.
Blinded and bruised, innocent.

We are such foolhardy neophytes,
the poets, and the flowers!
Rushing head over heels
into the sun. Our bodies, pages
upon which the light will unfold
the secrets of everything it holds.

Like children, stuffing pocketfuls
of treasure in our hearts, we offer
our measly gifts of words for love
or grace returned, while time withers
us, and the world too, takes all that it can.

Josie Di Sciascio-Andrews

Moon Birth

she has seen the black edge of night
birthing a blood orange moon
lighting up the sky with misty glow

magical, dark water woman
cradling a fair headed child

it was the face of love
she saw

the man in the moon

trailing flickering flames of memories
across dark waves

orange
red
yolk like a sun, moon

emerging out of sombre depths

the world's face glowed
as if for the first time,
beyond all dreams,
bursting illusions
with unexpected moon birth

like the night her children came
and the unknown took shape
beyond her will

blood alchemy of newborn skin, eyes, lips

celestial bodies' perfect form

emerging out of water
out of darkness

Josie Di Sciascio-Andrews

Blue Evening

tonight
the lake is a blue daiquiri

my heart a raw wound
waiting to be assuaged
by wind and waves

as if they could
cauterize the hollow
blood inlets
of my unrequited longing

Buddha, Jesus,
you
walking on water
at last

stretching out your hand
to save me

Your Return

The sound of your voice
makes the world
right again.

Stitches earth to sky.

All in order
As it should be.

Finally,
the moth-like, high rising
flight of seagulls
scatters glitter
within the vault of a rainbow.

Tiny white wings
dissolving past storms
into copper gilded blue.

A pot of gold.

Green meadow magic.
Love-luck your return.

The long awaited salve
to bind the ever rifting chasm
of my unbridgeable grief.

Josie Di Sciascio-Andrews

Summer's End in the Gardens of Bronte Pier

Another August of bitter green foliage surprises us
With its spill of crab apples on sidewalks.
Innocent exuberance hitting reason, hard.

In garden patches, the bruise of echinacea
Is bleeding purple hues into shades of dusk.

Galaxies of black-eyed Susan clusters aim
Their tarantula gazes towards space.
Mounds of multioptic nuclei centering in
On the cohesion of golden petals. Naively
Prepping themselves to an ochre wilt.

The skin of things inches forth
Into the clarity of evening. Undaunted
By the fear mongering mantra of wasps;
The overcrowded meccas of fruit flies hovering
Over the nectar of overripe fruit.

It is all so scientific. So purposeful,
This gratuitous, lustful reprieve
Of life' s slow bloodletting
Hypnotically easing the world to a fade.

Always the damned circling
Of mosquitoes in the dark
Under the crescent tilt
Of one more harvest moon
Blanching the lake's never ending heave
Of silverfish waves.

Again, the wind is coaxing nightly processions of sailboats
Back to the harbour. Sailors, silent and staunch
Like Doges are tying ropes to masts.
Dropping anchors in this little Venice laguna,
Where shadows and tree tops are my only cupolas.
The sun's remnant pyrotechnics, my only cherubim

Josie Di Sciascio-Andrews

Rimming the benevolent architecture
Of clouds. Setting the random
Stone throws of stars into effigies of Gods.

On the rocks, the lighthouse
Is cutting acute angles into the water.
Its constant throb, mirroring
the perfect geometry of my heart.
With its telltale alphabet
Strewn into the torpid pull
Of the crepuscular void.

This New Morning

the pale blue sky draws a tiny line
across the lake's grey eyelid

a seagull planes down
onto the wet pebbles

struts by a stone Inukshuk
built yesterday perhaps

by children playing on the beach
or two lovers, maybe
stacking dreams
stone upon stone like kisses

beyond the bark of the old oak tree
a large willow hangs on the edge

caressing the water's paleness
with long, green shimmers

this morning, the benches are witness
to this empty theatre
as my skin is to the shiver of cold wind

I stand here alone
a hazy figure sketched
against the muted colours of this still life canvas
still life
waiting to be painted on
with the bold strokes of some new meaning

while behind me
on the busy streets of town
life clanks like a chain of metal cans
rattling beyond all dreams
with its trail of truths and delusions

Josie Di Sciascio-Andrews

Saturday Afternoon Closing Time

At six o'clock
The mall's parking lot
Is eerily De Chíricoesque.

Amped to the max
The sun has bleached
All pavement to a bone.

And evening begins to fill
The angles of arches and doorways,
Lonely sprockets protruding
Their functional purposes
From large, empty walls.

One by one, cars are pulling out
From the yellow delineated spaces
That were abuzz all day
With spasmodic comings and goings.

Emptied,
The plaza unmasks
Its' Savannah face
Of soiled, parched surfaces.

Beside the trash bins,
In concrete planters,
Wind is blowing manes
Of ornamental trees,
Exotic grasses, tropical begonias.

Screaming crowds of seagulls
Are hovering upon the remnants
Of human harvest.
The frenzied food gatherings
In markets. Commerce of goods: elixirs, potions,
Scents and face paints for matings.
The accoutrements of survival.

Josie Di Sciascio-Andrews

For one more day.
One more cycle
On the paved landscape
Of this civilized wilderness.

In a precise, clockwork trickling,
Everyone has gone home for the night.
Recoiled to their habitations
Strung like leaves on branches
Of a thousand lamp lit streets.

I am left here alone to observe.
The animal in me finally free
To roam unimpeded
From the rightful entitlement
Of the herd.

Solitude.

Respite of the human.
Alone with a dream
Of the original idea of the possible:

That I am one.
That I matter.
That I am not replaceable.
That I am not obsolete.

Evolution

On the drives in my car
I have plucked every memory
from the roads of this town,
as if my repetitive meanderings
could have shucked them of all referents.

Everyone has come and gone.
Died. Been replaced.
Giving the illusion of continuity
To these suburban streets.

But nothing is the same.

Strangeness has moved in
Like a new neighbour.

It inhabits the old houses now.
Embodies the foliage of the old trees.
It has even settled in my own heart.

There are faces with new names
Looking out of the renovated doors.

They are pale, holy hosts
Exhalting a short lived sacredness
From gilded tabernacles.

Immigrants Fishing on the Oakville Pier

Tonight cold wind stitches the waves.
Gathers them up like crepe satin.
Threading flickers of light
Into their dark, jade depths.

Across the lake, white sails
Bite the sky's pale lip.
A regatta of shark's teeth
Aimed at the unsuspecting neck of night.

A few men are fishing on the pier.
Beyond the shimmering sound of chimes
I can hear the echo of their foreign tongues.

Their silhouettes etch strange shadows
In the deepening blue of evening.
Weave smoke signals to the constellations
With their cigarettes' burning glitter
That will fall like ashen skin at their feet
As they sit and wait with lines and nets
For a mythic catch that may not come.

The stars cannot birth the words.
The fish they hook will not speak
The language of their souls' longing.

Beside them, the lighthouse
Painted red like a woman's mouth
Drags its long white tip.

Exhales pulsating light into the night.
Beguiles with her trance of promise.

But there are no words tonight.

Silence spills from the bloody heart
Of this metal, painted whore

Josie Di Sciascio-Andrews

As she gives and gives in the dark
Forever pretending to rescue
The lost and the drowning.

Rain

It has been raining all day, all night
The rain has polished the roads to black opal
Mirroring streamers of uneven neon
In the billowing reflections of dark stone rivers.
The rain is doing its pointillism
Scattering cold diamond globules
On the needled tips of tall pines
Scouring the night like an old green jar.
The trees and their soggy shadows
Have become slippery squids,
Tentacles looming skyward,
Some of them blemished
With strings of malfunctioning lights,
Unsightly and irksome like aphids.
Wet spider webs
Hanging between branches
And telephone wires
Glisten
Drip tedium
Onto the wasted moments
That gather momentum
In puddles
In the cul de sacs
Of time and space
Bending
Around street corners
Their bright signs
Marking nothingness with names
Beneath tall lamp posts
That bow their heads
Like watchful sentinels of silence.
And it dawns on me
That maybe
The whole world is a giant spider web
Thread upon thread, spun
Into pathways of meaning.
Creation meandering

Josie Di Sciascio-Andrews

For its own sake
With its inherent calculations.
A universe to dwell upon
To be caught in
And that within it
I too am spinning
Filaments from my own wrists
Like blood
Like words
To grip tightly with at the edges
Of my abyss
Casting nets of ropes
To rest upon
To fall into, if necessary.
A safety net
Of sense and beauty
Sticky
Like a trap

Summer Evening

on the opalescent ripples
of the lake at dusk

geese are lining up
in haphazard formations

spelling cryptic meanings
like black messages in Arabic

the sky, drunk with summer
lifts a copper goblet
into the coming night
spilling sunset onto the dark spine
of Toronto's skyline
like so much crumpled tinfoil

on the other side, darkness
emits intermittent lights
on and off red
through the heavy foliage
of trees nestled along the horseshoe

hiding the Gotham like squalor
of Hamilton's industrial harbour

better here alone
on the rocks
in this hidden, silent cove

better here
under this large white moon
healer of my sins
this communion wafer
holy moon
threading an uneven line
from space to me
across the water

Josie Di Sciascio-Andrews

like the white seagull
hopping ever closer
on the algae covered stones
at my feet
with its carnivorous beak
its flat, fish eye
calculating to strike
perhaps to oust me
as if it sensed
the corpse in me
like some quantum premonition

Two Muskoka Chairs

Yesterday,
Searching through a box
Of old photographs,
I remembered
That summer the storm hit.

How it tore the trees
From their very pith.
Knocking them down on roads
And hydro wires. Blocking traffic
Through town. Creating outages.

I remembered how the wind had rocked
That rickety cottage, barely anchored
As it was to sand, on railway ties.

All night the rain had pelted
The asphalt shingles, shaking
The frail siding to its foundations.

It was a miracle the pine framed window panes held up.
The roof riding it out like an old canoe.
With its precious cargo of our children and us,
Two disparate oars, roaring to safety
From the storm. Inside.

The next morning, while everyone slept,
I had gone out in my robe, coffee in hand,
To assess the damage. Barefoot
Stepping carefully over the debris
Of acorns, leaves and twigs from a fallen oak
Littering the deck and everything.

On the barbecue, shucked from its pivot
The patio umbrella lay back, unhinged.

Josie Di Sciascio-Andrews

The two Muskoka chairs had made it through
Unscathed. Under soggy, gardenia-rose
Tropical patterned cushions
Beneath a disappearing hue or robin's egg blue.
Their weathered driftwood stood firm
Like stone. Stoic as wisdoms.

In the distance, from across the water
They must have etched Canada.
Kept watch over its silent face.
Parched with sun, wind and endless snows.
Withstanding it through to the limpid springs
Of loons and cold water lilies floating like open secrets.
Extrapolating light from their long drowned roots.
Deep in Precambrian rock and virgin forests.

Such dangers cupped in black tea coloured lakes!

I wondered then where passion was.
Reading Neruda, and love so far away.
Saying what? With whom?

While you, inside, scanned the newspaper
From front to back. Planned for retirement.
Watched hockey.

I remember drinking wine
Outside, after putting the kids to bed
And lighting lemon scented luminaries.
Braving the mosquitoes and the black flies
Before the big storm hit.

In the photo, I am young.
In my orange-turquoise sari,
Wild red flip-flops. Silver bangles.

I am sitting in one of the two
Empty Muskoka chairs.
My silhouette merging with the growing dark.
Staring at the moon.

Magical Woods

you could get lost in this
small view of peace

white on white on golden white
light permeating into copper shadows

here too is the soul of things

resting in the hidden corners
of unobserved places
too small to mention

the uneventful stories of tiny shrubs

small like the chambers of your heart
where no one has been for years

like you alone in your corner of the world

where beauty has come and gone
slipping away unobtrusively
without fanfare or notice

your beauty, like your love
such small events
in the scheme of things

yet how deep the glow
of light on snow bared roots

frozen blooms, hardy thistles
covered in ice crystals

infinitesimal magnification
of a larger universal design

Josie Di Sciascio-Andrews

here too is everything
you say

as you observe god like
the grand beauty of this small detail

this microcosm of wonder
here too is your soul

The Wild Things

Oh how the wild things grow!
Slithering tortuous and strong in the moonlight.

Suckling lymph with their tentacled roots
From the deep darkness of the moist earth.

Strong are the stalks
Of their snake like torsos.
The hairy spikes of their thistle spines.

It is so hard to pick them.

So much pain to endure
For just one precious, purple bloom.

Flowers of blood.

Cynical beauties.

Late bloomers
Adapted to self protect.

Twice bitten lovers
With malleable hearts.

I have seen the wild things grow.
Their shadows looming tall in the night.

Multiplying of their own volition.
In places beyond my reach.

How many times have I cut them down
Only to find them lush and thriving
Past my window in the morning?

I am getting used to their ever growing presence.

Josie Di Sciascio-Andrews

Tonight I can look beyond them
And still see the moon.

Tomorrow, like everything else,
I too will be of them.

Time Passage

We were so open
So wide eyed
In the morning.

Blue bells
Like children.

How much exuberance
Has been lost
In the midday sun.

New bloom's fluted edges
Drooping with futility.

Innocence tinged
With shades of death.

Josie Di Sciascio-Andrews

Petals

I have enshrouded
My griefs
Like a rose.

Shadows smudged
In the scented folds
Of days.

Poetic Incantation

a potion of magic
that's what this poem is
messages overflowing
from a dark cauldron
of flesh and bones
the odd glistening thorax
of furry legged spider
iridescent wing
of scorpion, belly up
in a throbbing brew
of hemoglobin, boiling
from veins, arteries
into central aortic vessels
red plated lozenges
sienna stained memes
lumping in the throat
from the hallowed grail
of a heart
buried deep
in a cage of ribs
carefully
I measure each utterance
add just the right spoonful
of noun, verb, adjective
the tiniest dash
of an article
stirring in the brew evenly
into smooth, glutinous consistency
as not to jar sensitive ears
with the sudden wrench
of a strident sound
beneath my stirring ladle
I can feel the twitching
of toad and snake
buckle,
nervous, I wince
at the sight of scales

Josie Di Sciascio-Andrews

and pupils bobbing
into view.
as I reshape death's rattle
into a broth of seamless skin
words perfect for casting spells
charming with proof of wizardry
a necklace of blood and bones
beads strung on filaments
of enchantment
a heart for pendant
a precious jewel
an amulet

The Surface of Things

Oh, how I walk on the surface of things!
Skimming the glass of mirrors,
While brewing deep
Below murky depths,
Invisible, chaos waits
To unravel me.

Seduced by the thrill of danger,
I glimpse below the sunlit patina
Of my reflection
Encircled by rippled light.

My soul luring to dive
Into the centrifugal centre
Of all things desired.

Is it not peace I seek?

Perhaps a new dimension.
Sequential regression
From ungraspable complexity
Into a simpler state
Of molecular suspension

In that mystical, foggy time
When atoms of my flesh
Had not collapsed
From waves to matter yet.

When no decisions had been made
In that unknown, forever time
When I did not exist.

Josie Di Sciascio-Andrews

Memories light up the landscapes of our nights like fireflies: places, loves,
children, friends lighting up our lives to defy despair.
Small tinder sticks of hope. Little miracles twinkling in the dark.

Fireflies in the Garden
Robert Frost

Here come real stars to fill the upper skies,
And here on earth come emulating flies,
That though they never equal stars in size,
(And they were never really stars at heart)
Achieve at times a very star-like start.
Only, of course, they can't sustain the part.

"Speech is but broken light in the depth of the unspoken."
George Eliot

Leaving

We are so much like the trees.

We mistake their stasis for imprisonment.
Our mobility for freedom.

But we too are deeply rooted.
Bound in place.

Conglomerates of electrons.
Atoms spinning ghost-like
Within the predetermined orbits
Of our hearts' metaphysics.

On the door of my house
There are no metal bars.

Unlike the trees, I escape daily
Though thousands of years
Of evolution keep me here.

Anthropology. Brain wiring.
Maternal instinct.

It all makes me think of a chunk of tree
I saw once. Trapped like flesh
Through a chain-link fence.

The tree itself, cut down.
No longer there.

Just this remnant torso
Of itself forever caught
Growing towards sunlight.

Escaping through steel.
Imagining it could.

Josie Di Sciascio-Andrews

Picking Lilacs at St. Mary's Pioneer Cemetery

In the cemeteries
The lilacs bloom.
By chance, in May
We found their fragrant, purple loot
Shading the forgotten stones. Their obelisks
Adorned with weathered cherubs, doves
Eternally poised for flight, riveted
Instead by Newtonian laws of physics
To the gravity of the mossy earth.
Mother called us delinquent
For entering a sacred place
To pick a few lilac branches.
Delinquent for grabbing
What little we could grasp
Of beauty, while we could.
Armfuls of sunlight
We gathered innocently
As we stood
Briefly
On sacred ground.

Glendella House*

a white star
painted on a window pane
is what remains
of Bill Hill's dream

a poem
of lake and sky

phlox
wild violet hues

tenacious beauty
reaffirming life's essence
upon the rubble
of a broken wall

such strange symbiosis
this gentling of nature upon history,

but soon, a new sturdy structure
will replace the chaos
of another era

the white star will shatter
under the blows
of a metal crane

and the pale blue shingles
of Glendella house
will vanish like ghosts
in Bronte's mists

the flowers too
will be upturned

purple blooms crowning rubble
replaced by clean, neat turf

Josie Di Sciascio-Andrews

*Glendella House was the home of Bill HIll, a founding business man of Bronte, Ontario. The house was moved and renovated. In its place they built a condo.

Thrift Shop

Once it was new.

Shone crisp on a glam
Black plastic mannequin
In a signature boutique.

Ticketed with an overpriced tag,
Exuded elusive utopias
Of ageless beauty. Style.

Now, it is here.

Jammed in endless
Rows of metal hangers
On endless racks
Of discarded garments.

Reduced below clearance
Value, it taunts
The hunter-gatherer
In me to unearth
Its hidden treasure.

A perfect gem.
Some remnant to be reclaimed
Of magic. Newness
Throbbing like a young heart
In a world of faded things.

Josie Di Sciascio-Andrews

Sleepless Night

at two in the morning
the moonlight
on the deep snow
kindles the shadows of bare branches
knobby fingers
on the white sheet below

the night sky
unusually light
veined with white clouds
pulls me
into the night
like foxes
running endlessly
on empty roads
strangely lit up
with cold, bright
winter solstice moon

I would hunt you down
in a dream
and never find you
your warmth elusive
like memories of summer
in another country
where chatter and laughter
bear no resemblance
to this winter night

Victoria Day Fireworks

it is breathtaking
this love
sparking in blue dusk
like fireworks

blasting off
in my heart
with the illusory excitement
of artificial stardust

thundering
with diamond explosions
in the cool night

love
falling like stars
in dark lakes of loneliness

I could keep it forever
a love like this

sparklers weaving excitement
in the dark
with promises of summer
on the exulted cusp of spring

may it never fizzle out
this love

may it reignite
forever like galaxies
in black space

to light our way
like bits of heaven
for our dark, lonely selves

Josie Di Sciascio-Andrews

Life Rounded Up

one
plus one
equals
the sum of its parts
two
sometimes drags
haloes
of remainders
points in time
dotting the shreds
of loves, places
bits damned
to repeat
the glitches
of broken promises
with their infinite minutiae
impeding
clear calculations
delete
only the digits
beyond our side
of point zero
matter
here
now
one
plus one
somehow
add up

Josie Di Sciascio-Andrews

One Meaning

So many words
Lose their meaning.

I seek the one
Pure sound
Of hope, love, life.

Everything else is detritus.
A cacophony of insignificance.
Words for the sake of rhyme.
Clever concoctions of the trite.

I want to imagine a world
Washed clean of rationalizations
People in harmony
Raked of the junk of skewed philosophies.

Stop displaying the gore of the killings.
Enough with the glorifications of error for profit.
Enough of the lessons never learned.

History, it seems, is the time line of the insane and the popular
The shockingly evil, the inhuman.

Give me a new page.

I want to stand barefoot.
A child in awe of an eclipse.
The ocean at my ear, in a sea shell.

Give me a pen and paper
Where I can doodle away the inhumanities of my time.
Safe from the squawking of the uninformed and the disillusioned.

Josie Di Sciascio-Andrews

Emerald City

Rebuilding the crumbling walls
Of a ruined Golden Age
Should be no quest for a child, nostalgic
For home. Kansas, beyond the vortex
Of windstorm, beast and witch
Dismembering the ideal with wily artifice;
Lulling a girl's resolve in poppy fields,
To awaken, finally wizened in a Quadling Kingdom
Dusting off the slumber from her limbs
To resume step after eager step
Along a winding road of yellow
Brick, strategically placed like crumbs
Leading her back like familiar words
To maps of return voyages, scrolls
Of merit from the wise, in glass towers up ahead.
Surely, her wide-eyed awe, her peasant braids,
Her blue gingham pinafore may have been construed
For bumpkin gullibility. "And should I, at your harmless innocence
Melt as I do?" Said the witch.* Arm in arm with an inconstant
Courage, an underrated brain and a gutbucket heart
Dorothy tore back the sash on a sham wizard.
"Click! Click!" Went the shoes. "Home!" Cried the heart.
"Just follow the road!" Said the brain. Her own words blinking
Like sunlit glass in her hands.
Like emeralds.
Keys to kingdoms.

* Milton, "Paradise Lost" Book 4

Josie Di Sciascio-Andrews

Recent Prizes and Awards

- First Place in the International Poetry Prize, Città del Galateo-Antonio De Ferraris, Verbumlandiart, Italy, for poets writing in English, for "The Sun Over Mississauga," 2023
- "The First Time I Heard Leonard Cohen" was nominated for the Pushcart Prize, 2022
- Honorable Mention in the International Poetry Prize, Città del Galateo-Antonio de Ferraris, Verbumlandiart, Italy, for poets writing in English, for "In Those Meticulous Rituals of Dressing in Our Sunday Best," 2022
- Honorable Mention for "On First Communion Day," Carmen Ziolkowski Poetry Prize, 2023
- Honorable Mention for "Toast, snow" in The Royal City Literary Arts Poetry Award, Westminster B.C., 2023
- Judge's Choice Award in the 2023 Dr. William Henry Drummond, Spring Pulse Poetry Contest, 2023
- Honorable Mention for "Jewel" and "Spring Storm" in the Spring Peepers Anthology Contest by The Ontario Poetry Society, 2023

Josie Di Sciascio-Andrews' poetry reviews have appeared in the following publications:

The League of Canadian Poets
Canadian Poetry Review
Pacific Rim Review of Books, Ekstasis Editions
Verse Afire
The Miramichi Reader
The Artisanal Writer
Arc Poetry Magazine

Poetry Readings and Essential Appearances

The Art Bar, Toronto
Howl Radio, University of Toronto
Eh Poetry Podcast, Ottawa
The Italian Cultural Institute, Toronto
The Columbus Centre, Toronto
Alliance Française, Toronto
The Oakville Arts Council
The Oakville Literary Café Series
Poetry & Prose, Oakville
The Oakville Public Library
The Burlington Public Library
The Mississauga Public Library
The Writers and Editors Network, Toronto
Namaashoum Poetry Radio, Ottawa
100 Thousand Poets for Change Event, Toronto
Litterateur's International Literature Conclave, Keynote Speaker, India
Short Story Today podcast, featured guest, New York
Accenti Magazine's Poetry on Zoom Event
Acta Victoriana Readings, University of Toronto
The Ontario Poetry Society, Oakville

Biographical Note

Josie Di Sciascio-Andrews is a poet, author, teacher, and the host and coordinator of the Oakville Literary Café Series. Her book of poems, *Meta Stasis,* was released in July 2021 by Mosaic Press and *A Jar of Fireflies* was first published by Mosaic Press in 2015. Josie's other books include *Sunrise Over Lake Ontario, Sea Glass, The Whispers of Stones, The Red Accordion, and Letters from the Singularity.*

Josie's poetry has been shortlisted for *The Malahat Review*'s Open Season Award, the Winston Collins/*Descant* Best Canadian Poem Prize, The Eden Mills Literary Contest, *Accenti Magazine* Poetry Contest, the Venera Fazio Poetry Contest, and the Dr. William Henry Drummond Poetry Prize. Her poetry won first place in the 2023 International Poetry Prize: Città del Galateo-Antonio De Ferraris in Italy.

In addition, some of her poems are featured on The Niagara Falls Poetry website and one of her poems was included in *Another Dysfunctional Cancer Poem Anthology* edited by Priscila Uppal (Mansfield Press, 2018*)*, which *Chatelaine Magazine* acclaimed as one of the best Canadian poetry books of 2018. In 2022, Josie's poem "The First Time I Heard Leonard Cohen" was nominated for The Pushcart Prize.

Josie is also the author of two non-fiction books: *How the Italians Created Canada*, which is about the contribution of Italians to the Canadian socio-historical landscape, and *In the Name of Hockey*, which offers an unflinching look at emotional abuse in boys' sports. Josie teaches workshops for Poetry in Voice and for Oakville Galleries. She writes and lives in Oakville, Ontario.